Climate, Suffering and Hope: the realities of a young person today

Rachel Jones

BookLeaf
Publishing

Presentation by *BookLeaf Publishing*

Web: www.bookleafpub.com

E-mail: info@bookleafpub.com

ISBN: 9789357740036

First edition 2023

The Broken World

When I was told of the broken world,
They said there was no need to worry.
'The scientists will fix it' they said,
'Besides, there's no real hurry.'

Yet soon after I learned that this was untrue,
That scientists, despite all their trying,
Could not keep up with the destruction we made,
That the world was already dying.

And then I learned that this in fact
Cannot be pushed aside,
That if we kept pretending,
I'd be killed as the earth died.

And so it seems it's down to me
to fight that I might live.
The situation's dire
So I'll give all I can give.

Here's the problem that haunts me
Again and again:
If we somehow do survive,
What will I do then?

Should I spend my life trying

To save the world I see?
Or should I plan for a future
That may or may not come to be?

Each way I feel as if
I've lost part of my life:
I constantly live in fear of the end,
In strife.

I know the end won't come next week,
Tomorrow, or today,
But ten years, or twenty,
That's not far enough away.

At the end of my life

Now I'm nearing the end of my life at the ripe
old age of twenty.
It's been pretty good to be fair, with much joy
and wealth and plenty.

Although, I fear that's partly why my life will be
so short.
In my time I've taken more than anybody ought.

I didn't truly mean to though, in fact I did not
know
That how we all were living caused destruction,
a shadow
Creeping up on us like a parasite, too small to
see, except
That science gave warning, so promises were
made, but none kept.

And so began the age of lies, with a powerful
few choosing
To gamble the future of humanity, knowing the
high chance of losing.
They invested millions on telling us not to care,
But no amount of money can make solutions
from thin air.

And now we're finally learning of the damage
we've incurred,
But they act like it's someone else's problem.
Are they absurd?

Can they not see that the world is burning from
their hideout?
Can they not hear millions of people crying out
For help from the very souls who condemned
them to this fate?
The people saved by the same decisions that
caused this disaster. Hate
Is there and in plentiful supply but overpowered
by desperation,
By millions of people seeking to avoid
annihilation.

So here we are, the end of my life at the ripe old
age of twenty.
It was preventable, but those with that power
chose a life of wealth and plenty.

Please!

I ask you to stop.
I beg you to stop.

I tell you we're dying.
I show you we're dying.

And yet you continue to kill us.
Money's worth more, so you kill us.

Why can't you see that despite it's worth,
Money's no use when we're dead,
When there's no one left on Earth.

I'm scared

I'm scared.
I've been brought up to believe in science,
To trust that it is true.

I'm scared.
The science says we're in danger of setting off
irreversible reactions across the planet, making it
potentially uninhabitable.

I'm scared.
This can be stopped but we need drastic action
now.

I'm scared.
The politicians know this and yet they do
nothing.

I'm scared.
The CEOs know this and yet they do nothing.

I'm scared.
I see drought in Africa and flooding in Pakistan,
And yet they do nothing.

I'm scared.

Wildfires are ravaging the world,
And yet they do nothing.

I'm scared.
Every summer is warmer that the last,
And yet they do nothing.

I'm scared.
I tell them I'm scared,
And yet they do nothing.

I'm scared.
I'm desperate.
I've done everything I can,
And yet they do nothing.

I'm scared.
I'm desperate.
I'm frightened.

I don't want to die.

Upon Reflection

When I was younger I thought,
If I did what I was taught,
The world would be free, with no work from me,
But from this only anguish was wrought.

A message for world leaders and CEOs

If you were offered money to kill your child,
would you do it?
Is there a price high enough to make you at least
consider?
I know this sounds absurd but I must ask since I
notice
That your actions condemn them, indirectly,
you're pulling the trigger.

The end of the world

Here it is, though far too soon,
It's caught us now: the end.
Cowering in the cold dark air,
No more can I pretend

That there's still hope for better days
That healing might still come,
But as I clutch my children tight
I know despair has one.

The metal box in which we cower
Is rattling and shaking.
Is it from the howling wind
Or is it the Earth that's quaking?

There's nothing left for us to do
But wait for her revenge.
We regarded her as nothing
Though in truth she was our friend.

We beat her, abused her,
Used her till she broke,
And our betrayal forced her
To take vengeance, to make us choke.

My children won't have happy lives.
I doubt they'll live at all.
Here at the end they shake with despair,
So helpless, so small.

And now I hear it approaching,
A great rumbling roar.
All this damage that we created,
What was it all –

The Forest

The trees are still.
The earth is solid.
Nothing moves.

And yet I hear the forest teaming with life.

The Sky

I don't like saying the sky's blue because it's so
much more.
It's a gateway to a world of colour we can never
fully explore.

It's a tapestry of every colour under the stars and
sun.
Every day a new display, unique, every one.

It's a system of navigation, used to travel in days
gone by.
It's the world's first clock and calendar, all this
is the sky.

It shows us a universe that's dark, cold and
empty.
But it also brings us warmth and light. It gives
us life a plenty.

The plea of a traveller

The world is so exciting,
There's so much to see.
If I spent my whole life travelling,
For more time I'd still plea.

People

People are beautiful,
And we are frightening.
We are intelligent,
And so very ignorant.

We are kind and gentle,
Understanding and polite.
We are cruel and judgemental,
Violent and vindictive.

We are capable of so much good.
We can go to space, save endangered species,
cure diseases.

But are also capable of truly evil acts.
Genocide. Warfare.
Ignoring those in need, turning our backs.

People are varied, everyone is unique,
And though it's scary, when I think of our
beauty my fear becomes weak.

To my best friend

I hope you know how much I love you,
Though I don't say it often enough.
You're always there through thick and thin,
My rock when times are tough.

I don't even need to let you know
What's going on with me:
You always know, as I do for you,
We give each other space, judgement free.

You know me better than I know myself,
You always put a smile on my face.
So I hope you know how much you're loved,
Truly, you are my safe space.

The elegy of a hero

How is the water so calm,
The breeze so light and warm?
And yet you lie before me, dead,
your body broken and torn.

Your sister sits beside me,
Shaking in pain.
She is but one of many you spared,
Your death was not in vain.

You died to protect your family
From your best friend who betrayed you.
And now we need to work out how
To carry on without you.

You, a sister, a daughter, a lover, a friend.
So much to so many, but now it must end.
It's not enough, but I promise I'll try
To tell of the sacrifice you made, so that we
would not die.

The song of a bard

Oh great Queen, to you I'm indebted,
Oh great defender, to our enemies dreaded.
A fierce warrior, you defend this land
From all those who seek it, their kingdoms to
expand.

Oh lover of music, you welcome bards such as I,
Give us freedom to create, to praise you on high.

All these things, though great, are not
unexpected
For a queen, such as you, who's so loved and
accepted.
But you have made many unusual choices
And shown that you hear all your people's
voices.
Of some of these things, I shall now relate
And explain why they are so remarkable and
great.

Firstly, tales of your courage shall be told.
You've fought with your army from fourteen
years old.
Though expected of your brother this was never
forced on you,

But now, of those able to defeat you, there are
few.

Many a battle you've fought and won,
Not resting, unrelenting, till the war is done.
Always fighting to protect and defend,
Never for gain, always peace you intend.

And peace you've created through this next
unique choice,
Proving you listen to everyone's voice:
You've legalised magic, and welcomed its
practitioners,
Giving them safety, not taking them as prisoners.
For you heard them as they cried out to your
father
That to have magic or not, you can't choose
which you'd rather.
In this land, where magic is uniquely accepted,
Even new magical knights you've created.

So kind and gentle is your heart
That the boarders are open to all, needy or smart.
Many, to move to this place, feel a call,
For in this land, you've created a safe haven for
all.

Dearest Imagination

Dearest Imagination,
Thank you for being here.
I don't think I can ever repay
All you've done for me, my dear.

Dearest Imagination,
You've been with me from the start.
We played together, made a world that's better,
So thank you, from the bottom of my heart.

Dearest Imagination,
We grew up as one,
And when the world seemed cold and dark
We escaped to a place filled with warmth and
fun.

Dearest Imagination,
With you I built a home,
A place that was safe, with many a friendly face,
A kingdom of our own.

Dearest Imagination,
You have saved my life.
When everything was falling apart
You were there, my escape from the strife.

Dearest Imagination,
I think we ought to share.
You've helped me through, you can help others
too,
We'll make life easier to bear.

So thank you, Imagination,
My dearest and oldest friend.
I'm privileged to spend my life with you,
Always, till the end.

Body Dysmorphia

I can't trust my own reflection
To show a true image of my complexion.
It scares me that the people I see
Are as different in looks as you and me.

Sometimes I see someone far too thin,
Who stares back at me with eyes too dim,
A sunken face that's far too pale,
Not a person, but a skeleton, a body about to
fail.

Shortly after I might look to be
Fuller, more muscular, altogether more healthy,
A rounder face with colour in my cheek,
A body with shape, not just angular and weak.

Then that same day, I'll glance in the mirror
And see someone who's rounder and softer and
bigger,
Chubby cheeks and a double chin,
I take up more of the space I'm in.

It scares me that how I look changes and won't
last,
Though I know my body can't do it that fast.

So mirror, please, I long to know
The image that I truly show.

Anorexia

I can't really explain it.
I'm not sure I understand it fully myself.
And I've lived it.

Not wanting to eat doesn't make any sense:
We need food to survive.
Not knowing what you look like doesn't make
any sense:
Just look in the mirror.

This is what I thought,
Before I lived it.
It's hard not to think that,
Unless you've lived it.

It's not about what you look like,
Not really.
It's not just a plea for attention,
Not really.

It's about wanting to feel in control of
something,
when you've got no control in your life
You want to be attractive, because attractive
people look happy,

like they're in control of their life.

You fully invest in this one goal,
giving more than everything you've got.
Soon you're worth becomes dependant on this
one goal
Until it takes more than everything you've got.

You over analyse yourself so much
That you don't know what's real and what's
imagined.
You over analyse other people's reactions to you
So you don't know what's real and what's
imagined.

You're tired and cold all the time.
You're hungry all the time.

But eating makes you a failure.
It makes you worthless.

It doesn't make sense,
And you know it.
You're still not in control,
And you know it.
This is worse than before,
And you know it.

But to stop would be giving up that hope of
control,
Accepting that you are and always will be
worthless, a failure.

Asexuality

I am different:
My relationships don't fit the norm.
I am different:
I sometimes feel broken and perverted.
I am different:
The way I see the world is not like most.
I am different, but I'm hidden.

I am hidden:
My relationships can appear normal.
I am hidden:
Many others who are different say that I'm not
different enough.
I am hidden:
I have never had to fight for the right to live as
me.
I am hidden because I'm asexual.

I am asexual:
Intimacy is painful and extremely discomforting.
I am asexual:
I laugh when my friends get distracted by
crushes.
I am asexual:

I desire close relationships with people, just the
same as most.
I am asexual.
But I'm still me.

I am me:
I love to travel and learn about the world,
I am me:
I have an intensely creative soul,
I am me:
I am different, but I'm hidden.
I am me:
I'm asexual, and I'm free